GW00776524

Read*ux*

Readux Books: Series 1, № 2

Originally published as
"Der Verdächtige" and "Von der Lebenslust"
in *Spazieren in Berlin* in 1929
by Verlag Dr. Hans Epstein, Leipzig and Wien

First English translation, 2013

ISBN: 978-3-944801-01-8

Cover illustration by André Gottschalk
Design by Susann Stefanizen

Published by Readux Books
Sorauer Str. 16, 10997 Berlin, Germany

www.readux.net

In Berlin
Day and Night in 1929

Franz Hessel
Translated from the German by Amanda DeMarco

The Suspect

Walking slowly down bustling streets is a particular pleasure. Awash in the haste of others, it's a dip in the surf. But my dear fellow citizens of Berlin don't make it easy, no matter how nimbly you weave out of their way. I always catch wary glances when I try to play the flâneur among the industrious. I believe they take me for a pickpocket.

The swift, firm big-city girls with their insatiably open mouths become indignant when my gaze settles at length on their sailing shoulders and floating cheeks. It's not as if they had anything at all against being looked at. But the slow-motion gaze of the harmless observer unnerves them. They notice that with mine, there's nothing "behind!" it.

No, there's nothing behind it. I'd like to linger at first sight. I'd like to capture or recover the first sight of the city in which I live…

In the quieter outlying districts, incidentally, I'm no less of a spectacle. There, in the northern

5

part, is a square with a wooden scaffolding, the skeleton of a market, and right beside it, the widow Kohlmann's general merchandise shop, which also has rags; and above the bundles of wastepaper, bedsteads, and pelts, on the slatted veranda of her shop, there are pots of geraniums. Geraniums, pulsing red in a sluggish gray world, which I'm compelled to gaze into for a long time. The widow gives me the evil eye. She doesn't have the nerve to complain, maybe she thinks I'm an inspector; something's amiss with her papers for all one knows. But I mean well with her, I'd like to ask her about her business and her views on life. Now she sees I'm finally going across the way, where the cross-street starts, to stare at the backs of the children's knees as they play at hitting a ball against the wall. Long-legged girls, enchanting to watch. They hurl the ball back by turns with their hands, heads, and chests, twisting as they do so, and the hollows of their knees seem to be the center and origin of their motions. I feel the merchandise-widow craning her neck behind me. Will she notify the law about the kind of fellow I am? Suspicious role of the observer!

When twilight falls, old and young women lean at the windows, propped up on pillows. I feel for them what psychologists dispatch with words like "empathy." But they won't allow me to wait with and next to them for something that isn't coming, only to wait without object.

Street merchants who peddle something with a cry have nothing against it if you linger by them; but I'd rather stand next to the woman with a great deal of hair from the previous century slowly spreading her embroidery across blue paper and staring mutely at the customers. And I'm not really one of them, she can hardly expect that I'd buy anything from her wares.

At times, I'm wont to go into the courtyards. In old Berlin, life beyond the courtyard buildings becomes denser and more profound, making the courtyards rich, the poor courtyards with a bit of green in one corner, the carpet rods, the garbage cans and the pumps left over from the time before running water. Ideally, I manage to go mid-mornings, when singers and violinists emerge, or the organ-grinder man, who also regales us with nature's pipe on his free pair of fingers, or the wonder who plays the snare in front and the kettledrum in back (a cord runs from a hook on his right ankle to the kettledrum on his back and the pair of bells on top of that; and when he stomps, a mallet dashes against the kettledrum, and the bells crash together). Then I can stand next to the old porter woman—or rather the doorman's mother, old as she looks, and as accustomed as she seems to sitting on her little camp chair. She takes no offense at my presence, and I'm allowed to look up into the courtyard windows, where young type-writer-ladies and sewing girls from the offices and workshops crowd to see the concert. They pause, blissfully entranced, until some bothersome boss comes and they have to shuffle back to their work. The windows are all bare. Only one, on the second-to-top floor, has curtains. A birdcage hangs there, and when the violin sobs from the bottom of its heart and the barrel organ wails resoundingly, then the canary starts to warble as the only voice from the silently staring windows. It's beautiful. But I also like to get my share of the evening in these courtyards, the children's last games—they're called to come upstairs again and again—and the young girls who come home and want to leave again; I alone find neither courage nor pretext to intrude; it's too easy to see I'm unauthorized.

Around here, you have to have to, otherwise you're not allowed. Here you don't walk, you walk somewhere. It's not easy for the likes of us.

I can count my blessings that a pitying friend sometimes allows me to accompany her when she has errands to run. To the stocking repair shop, for example, where a sign on the door reads: "Fallen stitches taken up." In this dreary entresol, a hunchback scurries through her musty, wooly room, which is brightened by new glossy wallpaper. Goods and sewing supplies lie on the tables and étagères, around porcelain slippers, bisque cupids, and bronze statuettes of girls, the way herding animals gather around old fountains and ruins. And I'm allowed to have a close look at all of it, and learn a piece of city and world history from it, while the women confer.

Or I'm taken along to a mender who lives on the ground floor of a courtyard building on Kurfürstenstraße. A curtain, which doesn't quite reach the floor, divides his workroom from his sleeping quarters. On a fringed scarf hanging over the curtain, Kaiser Friedrich is colorfully depicted as crown prince. "That's how he came from San Remo," says the mender, following my gaze, and then goes on to show me his other treasures of monarchist loyalty: the last Wilhelm, photographed and very much framed with his daughter on his knees, and the famous picture of the old Kaiser with children, grandchildren, and great-grandchildren. He's glad to resew my lady-republican's green jacket, but at heart he keeps, as he says, "with the old lords," especially as the Republic only cares for the young people. I don't try to convince him otherwise. My political insights are no match for his objects and objections. He's very friendly with my friend's dog, which sniffs around at everything, curious and always on the trail of something, just like me.

I like to go walking with this little terrier. We both get completely lost in thought; and he gives me occasion to stop more often than would normally be allowed such a suspicious person as myself.

Recently, however, things took a bad turn for us. I picked him up from a building where we were both strangers. We went down a set of stairs in which a grillwork elevator shaft had been installed. The elevator was a grim interloper in the once serenely wide stairwell. From the colorful windows, bulky heraldic ladies stared incredulously at this traveling dungeon. And their grips loosened around the jewels and emblems in their hands. Surely it smelled very discrepant in this ensemble of various epochs, which distracted my companion to such a degree from present surroundings and customs that on the first step of the steep staircase, which led down to the foot of the elevator cabinet from the mezzanine, he—forgot himself! Such a thing, my friend later assured me, could only happen to such a civilized creature in my presence. That I could put up with. I was hit harder by the accusation made by the building's porter at the moment of the embarrassing event, and who, unfortunately, stuck his nose out of his loge just as we were forgetting ourselves. In proper recognition of my complicity, he turned not to the pup, but to me. Pointing with a gray menacing finger at the site of the misdeed, he barked at me: "Eh? Anya wanna be a cultured yuman bein?"

Lust for Life

Our youths learn how to enjoy things, which to the German generally doesn't come naturally. In his zeal for pleasure, the Berliner of yesterday still lapses into the dangers of accumulation, quantity, of the colossal. His coffee houses are establishments of pretentious refinement. Nowhere the cozy, unremarkable leather sofas, the quiet corners, as the Parisians and the Viennese love them. Instead of saying waiter, he still calls after the stupidly titled *Herr Ober*, simple ground coffee is called a *Mokka double*, fifty barmaids at the counter are more than ten. New "Grand Cafés" are always being founded with room for around a thousand guests. On the ground floor there's a Hungarian ensemble, on the second floor, two bands oblige the dancers. First-class personnel provide the audience with diversion during the breaks in dancing. "Peculiar" lady orators take the stage. The ads and notices promise international attractions, a cosmopolitan establishment, etc. Yes, you surely do get something for your money. "With free entry and 3 marks' purchase you'll enjoy Germany's best cabaret uninterrupted from 8½ to 12½. Afternoon refreshment 2 M 50 with cake, as much as you'd like."

Business, business! Even the old-fashioned souls always want to join in.

Once in your life, you must experience the day after Christmas in a monster establishment, when all and sundry go out, because the help has the day off anyway. Then daddy really gets bold with the bill. And some things that are billed as bold can be had for pretty cheap. There are good mixed platters of hors d'œuvres, with everything included, lobster and caviar and artichoke hearts and all of it always for two people; double portions, like the gigantic entrecôte garnished with just a side of vegetables. There are first-class dessert platters. Nothing is lacking. Of course the son, sitting quietly bored next to his sparingly clad mother, already knows that it's finer to order something choice, and perhaps he'll find the opportunity to impress his elders with his special selection. He's more nonchalant toward the waiter than his father is. He'd rather be sitting over by those two unaccompanied young ladies. They may well be typists, going out alone today in spite of the men. They order very tastefully: French vegetable platters, *chicorée* and *laitu braisé*, only cocktails as an accompaniment, and afterwards table water with the meringues. He glances across at them and learns. The back of his head is shaved in the American style, but no roll of fat back there like his father has…

The monstrous, gigantic double concerts that the capital city puts on for the tongue, eye, ear, and dancing foot can't lay a finger on the new youth, our new Berlin girls. As far as eating, drinking, and smoking go, they have a few new methods, charming forbearances, hygienic mortifications, athletic precepts. They steer themselves through the crush of pleasures as assuredly as through that of the streets, finding a few paths for dancing among the thick of human masses, know which hotel or locale you can still dance in afternoons if need be, and have their cocktail parties where one dances in private company. It's admirable how they master Berlin's *Karneval*, which notoriously doesn't end with Shrove Tuesday and Ash Wednesday, but goes on for weeks uninterrupted. And there are nights with three or more important parties, one in the halls of the "Zoo," one at the Kroll Opera, one in the Akademie zu Charlottenburg, one in the Philharmonie, and, on top of that, a more intimate and particularly tantalizing one in this atelier or that. They know how to pick them, they know where the best band is playing, they invent clever itineraries to accomplish more. Above all else they're out for good dancing. The right dance partner is a very important figure, and not to be confused with whomever you love at the moment. His task is a completely different one. My young lady friends have informed me on this point while putting themselves together for one party or another. This preparation, this *Débarquement pour Cythère* is a significant moment, and for us observers, it is sometimes more instructive than the party itself. You must see their earnest expressions in the mirror as they bronze their arms and shoulders, "make up" their faces, try out turbans and feathered caps. They don't rush, they diligently add the final touches to the evening's work, like an artist who wants to create something lasting. They invent wonderful forms midway between a masquerade costume and an evening dress, innocent nakednesses, enticing concealments, and grotesque exaggerations in which to hide themselves away. Meanwhile you can enjoy their presence in peace, which otherwise isn't easy. Because they generally keep the tempo of their Berlin, which leaves the likes of us somewhat breathless. It's astounding how many locales and people they can take care of in an evening without growing weary. "Now let's go have an apéritif," they say suddenly, when tea time has grown a bit too dreamy. "Apéritif?" I ask bewildered, "I thought that didn't exist in this country." "Once again you underestimate our city's mettle," I'm scolded. And before I know it, I'm sitting in the car next to the quickest of them, as she drives down Budapesterstraße, past the glass atriums where the "smartest" domestic and foreign cars lounge, and stops across from the dinosaurs that are chiseled into the walls of the aquarium. We traipse over the glass plate at the entrance to the hotel, the glowing plate with the paradisiacal inscription. In the lobby, Maria (she demands that her friends call her that, to spite the laughable Marys, Miezes, and Mias of her set) exchanges a few words with the young poet who will soon make an appearance in film, and inquires after the health of their mutual friend, the boxer who sat out for so long. But the boy who hurries up to them with something to tell, posthaste, is the newest hope of the cabaret. Maria cuts things short and pulls me on. In the lobby of the bar, in the exedra, so to speak, groups of men in conversation sit on sofas lining the walls, and if I were better informed, I would recognize certain politicians or stock traders. We step into the pleasant lower room with the red ceiling beams. We would have liked to have taken our places on the high stools at the bar, but they're all occupied. And so Maria has to inform me from our table, who the slim man in the nice sand-colored shirt speaking English there at the next table is, and who his companion with the side-whiskers is. Maria is greeted by the young attaché's table. And the sweet creature she swiftly kissed while brushing past, that was the new little wonder of the revue, whom I recognize from pictures in the magazines. Right next to us sit two girls, both a little too freshly painted. Maria thinks she saw the one on the right in St. Moritz. "And why is the one on the left wrinkling her nose for the second time?" "One does that a great deal now. [She names an actress] did it on the stage. It's in vogue."

Roundabout the tables, whispers fly like in the best of Europe. That is, in the new Berlin one doesn't speak as loudly as in the old one. It's like you're at a reception here. But Maria doesn't allow more than a quarter-hour's sojourn. She has a

16

rendezvous for an early dinner at the Neva Grill with friends who want to go to the "Komödie" afterwards. She gives me over to one of her friends, who is supposed to take me to Restaurant Horcher. That's where she wants to meet us in an hour. "You can eat and drink Burgundy there with manly languor and distinction. I'll make it for dessert."

The sole, which my table-mate Gert, following a consultation with the son of the house, had decided upon and assigned to me, was prepared before our eyes in the good Parisian fashion. Over a Nuit Saint-Georges, I let Gert, who in his youth was already a respected man in banking and diplomatic circles, tell me about Berlin society. A concept that's hard to grasp and to delimit. The old divisions between the estates are ever-crumbling. Of course there are still a few ill-humored nobles in Potsdam and on country estates, mourning for the heyday of exclusive court society. But it's precisely the most genteel among them who seek to connect with the new times. Hospitable houses unify art and the haute bourgeoisie, and at the tables of great bank barons, socialist delegates meet with princes of former ruling houses. The big athletic clubs establish a new attitude, which excludes the heel-clicking of former guard lieutenants and the gallantry of the old students' corps. With youthful enthusiasm, the ambitious Berliner plunges into this new conviviality, and the ministers and the secretaries have to attend more strategic dinners than is ultimately good for politics. We come to the topic of women, and just as Gert was telling of a dinner party where he sat between two of them, of which the one on the right wanted to be prudently and properly regaled, while the one on the left tried for a double entendre in every second remark, or even brought up topics that would have made our mothers blanch with shame—in walked Maria, who seemed to us like the young queen of a new nation of Amazons, for whom the old concept society no longer existed. She isn't interested in continuing our theoretical discussion, but rather just wants to pick us up in time to get to an important film out from Russia. Gert really wanted to see the one by the Parisian American that was made using only a few objects from the studio, shirt collars, and hands. But Maria already knows that one from her last stay in Paris. She saw it in the small theater at the Ursulines in the Latin Quarter.

After the cinema, we sit downstairs in the Casanova, not far from the piano, where a composer famous for a hit song plays it nightly and sings. Gert and Maria deliberate on what else we could undertake to do. "Why don't you young people go upstairs and dance?" I ask. "I don't want to," says Maria, "but maybe Gert would find some companionship in the Blaue Salon." "Actually I was supposed to stop in to Ambassadeurs today at midnight." In my inexperience, I am informed that this is the newest extension of the Barberina. Gert and Maria then discuss the quality of the various jazz bands and tango groups in the big hotels, in the Palais am Zoo, in the Valencia, etc. I somewhat timidly introduce my experiences from the little Silhouette. "Why don't we just go across the way here to Eldorado? That's where the real bedlam's at. You're all for chaos, smoking and sport jackets, transvestites, little girls, and great ladies, aren't you? Of course you're more for what's proper, Gert, you want elegant dancing and limits, you want to go to Königin." But in the end we decide on something completely different.

A single light on the darker stretch of Lutherstraße. A few private cars before the door. The narrow hallway to the lobby is already overcrowded. A friendly manager extends the promise of accommodations. And at the door to the next room, the master of the house shakes our hands. It's useful to assure his personal protection for oneself, for, as I'm told, far from everyone is welcome here. That is to say, a man may come in and eat and drink, but if his nose displeases the owner of this strange inn, he doesn't allow the waiter to accept any payment, but rather approaches the alien's table himself, and requests that he consider this evening a treat on the house—and not to come again. Thus, it's a select clientele here. Heads of industry and culture! And shoulders! And eyebrows. There in the corner sit both the agreeably voluptuous woman and the slimly smiling one who sang at the revue about best friends. And near the piano— impressive even as a silent observer—the red-haired mistress of the grotesque. She bursts out laughing, as across from her the fat colossus from the North Sea coast, who pours out German poetry during the day and foreign drinks at night, bellows his well-known war cry, with which he's accustomed to ring in the second, merrier half of his evening. But the neighbors give a gentle shh! For presently, standing on the piano, her head ducked near the ceiling, a petite person in a sailor blouse gestures as she prepares for the song about the maidens of Camaret, which she is about to sing. She sings in French like her countrywoman, her idol in Montparnasse. And anyone who's spent enough time in Paris understands the song's dangerous words, which now rise into a sort of ecclesiastical melody. The others smile along, clueless and thankful. We were listening as we stood in the throng. Then we got seats in a corner at the bar. I look about while Gert and Maria dance. The few people I personally know who are possessed of art and lust for life are nearly all here. Gently booming, a stentorian voice calls me by my first name. It belongs to the man who once turned a little corner restaurant in Paris into the "Dôme," and who is now a famous painter here. In fact, I also know the beautiful Russian edging in next to him. He grants her his generous presence and observes through critical eyeglasses a pair of youths, literature's latest, sitting across from him in a reverent group. The slow, sympathetic smile on the abbot-faced man, who captured the better part of German and foreign literature in his *Bestiarium*, is addressed toward the two grown poet's daughters whom he watched play as children, and who've become world-travelers and conqueresses in the meantime. A new batch of arrivals forces their way through the narrow corridor of dancers, and, peeling themselves out of their coats, American and Asian Indians of both sexes emerge, at least insofar as they can be differentiated. They've come from a party, and before they're on to the next, they come to us, and want to seduce us into coming with them. Oh, the tinkling bracelet around Puck's leg, oh, the eagle feather over Sonja's hair! But we're staying. The young bartender is too good a host. We stay until—suddenly—it's three o'clock and some of the chairs are already standing upside-down on the tables. Maria still wants to take us to the ladies' club around the corner, but I'm out of luck there. Even today, when we belong to a member's retinue, its gates remain closed to us. But Gert gets us into Künstler-Eck unimpeded, where we spoon up a splendid chicken soup under gothic vaults. And now we can move on into the dawning day. Schwannecke still has a side entrance open for their gang. And what's more, Gert knows an association for restaurant employees that opens its doors in the middle of the night and serves food and drink until noon. He's a member there too. We could sit there between the night's last departers and the day's first comers, between singers and waiters, actresses and charwomen. But that's enough for today. Knowing that you could keep going for a long time lulls a body so pleasantly.

I've often noticed certain newspaper advertisements and placards carried by publicity men: "Little Walter the soul-soother with the golden heart, Berlin's best-known life of the party... Meeting point for broken hearts, once again daily... Widows' ball for older youths in the magnificent Reception Hall Ackerstraße…Traditional German ball, older youths only, lively ball music…Little Claire's stately widows' ball is the talk of the town. The elite only meet on Auguststraße." Sometimes it's condensed to: Elite widows' ball, where elite may refer to the widows or to the ball. The one on Elsässerstraße reads, "High-class ladies, no admission for gentlemen under 25." Indeed there isn't. I've observed at the entrance of such a dance palace how one boy wanted to show his papers as evidence of his maturity, but the man at the till rejected him contemptuously, saying, "We can see for ourselves!" And didn't let him in.

Since I visibly possessed the necessary age, I recently ventured to attend such a ball for older youths, I think it was in the Kaiser-Friedrich-Straße in Charlottenburg. I was with people who ordered a bottle of wine "delivered" to the table. Samos, I believe, was the unhappy choice. That made an impression. With a polite "Surely, I shan't disturb," the director of the event sat down with us. He wore a frock coat, similar to the one which our professor ordinarius from the 10th grade wore threadbare during the winter semester. The club, he said, was yet new, just about to establish its bylaws. This building, as it were, once belonged to a Free Mason lodge, which Kaiser Friedrich himself had dedicated. We could still see the rings painted on the walls from their lodge days. Back then this was a ceremonial hall. (It's true, there were, under toasts of the sort that you read on beer mats, really such rings.) And below, where the Evangelical Society GmbH is now lodged, once stood the coffin for the oath.

He jumped up and, together with a distinguished lady with heavy embroidery on her silk dress and somewhat unevenly fat legs, led a polka mazurka. Several couples could perform this historical dance without needing to look at the movements of the couple dancing before them. After that, the founder of the club came to us again and informed us that he was employed during the day as a craftsman (as he put it), and that by founding the club he intended to promote cordial and neighborly camaraderie among men. Disruptive elements who, for example, might overstep their bounds with a lady, should be eliminated. (We were too unfamiliar here to risk something of the sort.)

In the meantime, the man who had actually been hired to lead the dancing commenced the so-called Ice Skate Dance. He was gaunt, and what he was wearing was a swallow-tail coat. At certain turns in this dance, his partner clapped her hands once sharply and the others imitated her. But the leader of the dance just made an elegant flourish with his right hand. Some couples had an exceedingly dainty manner of holding each other, with splayed fingers and high elbows. Some gentlemen had placed a handkerchief between their hand and the lady's back. I made the observation that the more advanced the gentleman's youth was, the lower his hands drifted down the lady. Were these "elements"? Ladies who danced together did not exhibit the intimacy we know from certain venues, but rather ironized the odd coupling with glances and gestures. It was often ladies' choice, during which the ladies who happened to be free could "cut in"—as the experts put it—and take away any other lady's partner. It came down to some pretty courteous moments.

Once you've become a member, the club director informed us, the wardrobe also becomes cheaper. Then he rose again to give a brief oration, in which he stressed the merits of the traditional German dances, and called on the ladies and gentlemen present to display cordiality. The band offered up a prosit to this cordiality as they received fresh beer.

After this experience, I formed an opinion of the balls for older youths, which nonetheless seem to play a certain role in the life of Berlin. You're sure to find friends there. Socially, perhaps they're of similar effect to the matchmaking institutes whose announcements one reads in the newspapers and on notices pasted to buildings. Now when I read: "Round dances except Mondays, Thursdays and Fridays reverse ball," I understand.

The balls at which connections are made via so-called table telephones seem to aspire to fewer sociomoral designs. They occasionally also have hanging fountains and always something that their advertisements call "terrifically merry masses of visitors." They promise something "magnificent," "artistic," "intimate." They take place in the "most cultivated luxury locations in the world" on glass flooring, near the "High Life Bars" and "exquisite restaurants." In the most famous of these extensively lit ballrooms, there is a wonderful combination of water and light, in revolving, color-changing basins. According to the brochure, these marvels of water and light are not only tasked with pleasing the eye and elevating the mood, they also provide for the circulation of fresh air. The invention of the table telephone is very psychological: you see, the median Berliner is hardly as self-confident as he would like to seem. But on the telephone, he screws up his courage (The telephone is very befitting of him, after all. Instead of "farewell," nowadays he's accustomed to saying "Well, then ring me up sometime," or "I'll call you in the next few days.") and then he's reaffirmed by the management's appeal written in verse, which he finds in the interesting brochure:

Don't be bashful, ring her up,
You'll see if she likes you soon enough.

Yes, the ballroom is, as the new Germany's most popular verb expresses, completely "focused" on its guests.

In the half-light of tinted lamps hanging in a number of smaller halls and rooms in the North as well as the West, couples of the same sex circulate, here the girls and there the lads. Sometimes the girls are dressed, in a more or less enjoyable manner, as men, the lads as ladies. Their drives, once bold protest against the dominant moral laws, have with time become a rather harmless pleasure, and visitors who like to dance with the opposite sex are also allowed into these mellow orgies. They find a particularly favorable environment here. The men learn new nuances in tenderness from the female cavaliers, their partners from the masculine ladies, and your own normality becomes a peculiar stroke of luck. Oh, and the light fixtures are positively stirring. You see wooden or metal lanterns there with serrated frames, reminiscent of the fretwork of our boyhood.

Before, it seems to me, everything must have been more sinful. Apparently, matters of desire back then were more calibrated to their level of danger. Where today Reinhardt's chamber plays offer distinguished artistic endeavors, a steaming violet and golden dance hall once stood. There, before our shocked young eyes, tall corseted figures twirled in threadbare ball gowns with bosoms that were sometimes bare to the nipples, veiled and accentuated by tulle. Crackling petticoats tormented our senses, and when, to a somewhat clumsy can-can, skirts were gathered and shrill voices sang the hit tune about the peach on the tree, we became ill at ease. Wiser fellows found something for the heart in the ballrooms of the outlying districts, in Südende and Halensee, where good girls with principles and careers outnumbered the so-called "rejects." They had hands washed to redness and peculiar violet perfumes in constant conflict with nature.

Those were the days when the Palais de Danse bloomed for the extravagant among us in the city.

There, the ladies were Babylon and Renaissance, with certain pre-Raphaelite embellishments and variations. Some of them—who in those bygone days arrived in droshkies or automobiles from the Bavarian Quarter, pressed the money for the coachman or chauffeur discerningly into the porter's hand, and took a seat on the stools at the bar—pursued careers. Bakers' daughters became duchesses. One is supposed to have even made it to royal heights, though in society she didn't achieve the same degree of "reçue" as the new countesses and duchesses. Now, you wouldn't recognize this Palais today. What did I see when I recently made the mistake of stumbling in? Some lively, lusty people from Meseritz or Merseburg, had "gone out" with Berlin relatives they were visiting, expecting to see half the world, but only a declining, timid quarter turned up…

BERLIN - THE SLOW WAY

In the same way that the Slow Food revolution has created a compelling antithesis to the burgeoning Fast Food business, Slow Travel encourages people to resist "Fast" Travel – the frustratingly frequent habit of speeding through all the best known landmarks of a city in 24 or 48 hours – then leaving again. Slow Travel encourages us to slacken our pace, re-consider our motivations (and itineraries) and embrace a "less is more" instead of a "fast is better" ethos. It emboldens us to take pause. To think. To saunter instead of rush and enjoy the details instead of blurring past them.

We aim to facilitate any quest to get beneath the skin of the city a little, or discover it at a more leisurely pace. We offer an insider's view that will doubtless overlap from time to time with other Berlin travel sites, but will ultimately provide a unique and above all reliable resource that gives a broader, deeper perspective. We love this city and we want you to love it too.

www.slowtravelberlin.com

Franz Hessel

Franz Hessel was born in 1880 to a Jewish banking family and grew up in Berlin. After studying in Munich, he lived in Paris from 1906 to 1914, moving in artistic circles in both cities. His relationship with the fashion journalist Helen Grund was the inspiration for Henri-Pierre Roche's novel *Jules et Jim* (later filmed by François Truffaut). Their son Stéphane went on to become a diplomat and author of the world-wide bestselling *Time for Outrage!* In the 1920s and 1930s, Hessel worked as an editor at Rowohlt Verlag in Berlin. Simultaneously, he wrote novels and essays, which were widely praised for their poetic style. He also translated two volumes of Proust's *À la recherche du temps perdu* into German together with Walter Benjamin, as well as works by Casanova, Stendhal, and Balzac. In 1938, he fled with his family to Paris, then to Sanary-sur-Mer. In 1940, he and his son Ulrich were sent to the internment camp Les Milles. Franz Hessel died in early 1941, shortly after his release from the camp.